NOTEBOOK DOODLES®
HAPPY OCEAN

Jess ♡ Volinski

This book belongs to:

TO JOEY —
ALWAYS BE YOUR
ONE-OF-A-KIND, AMAZING
CREATIVE SELF!!

3/2022

Be Yourself to Be Creative

The thing I love most about art—making it myself or enjoying others' creations—is that **art allows you to be yourself by expressing yourself.** Whatever you love, whatever is important to you, whatever makes you who you are should come out in your art. By making art that matters to you, you're starting a conversation with everyone who sees it. You're saying, "Hey! This matters to me. What do **you** think about it?"

You might be wondering, how exactly do I express myself with art? That's where **The Elements of Art** come in. You might remember these from art class. Just like writers use words to tell a story, artists use these visual elements to express themselves and start their art conversation. All visual art—whether it is a painting in a museum, storyboards for a movie, a pattern on a bag, or a coloring book page—uses some combination of these seven basic building blocks of art. Not all art has to include all seven elements, but most art will include a few.

The Elements of Art

A **line** is formed as the connected distance between two points. Lines can be thick or thin, straight or curved.

Space refers to the areas in a piece of art that are around or within different parts of the art. There are two kinds of space: negative (space around areas), and positive (space within areas).

A **shape** is a defined area of space—a circle, square, blob, or a flower petal are all shapes.

Texture refers to the way the art physically feels when touched, or how an artist visually makes the art **look** like it would feel. Shading with pencils is an example of this type of visual texture.

Something has **form** if it has volume (or creates the illusion of volume). A three-dimensional sculpture has form. A two-dimensional drawing with shading that makes it appear three-dimensional can also have form.

Color is created when light hits an object and is reflected to our eyes. A color can be described with three properties: hue (the color's name, such as "red"), value (how light or dark the color is, also called a tint or shade of the color), and intensity (how vivid or dull the color is).

Value refers to the relationship between light areas and dark areas in a piece of art.

The Elements of Art IN ACTION

Let's look at one of my doodles and see what Elements of Art are here. Even though this is just a simple black and white drawing, it has line, shape, and space. When you color it in, you'll probably add form, color, value, and maybe even texture. That's all seven Elements of Art—on a coloring book page! How cool is that?! Art truly is all around us!

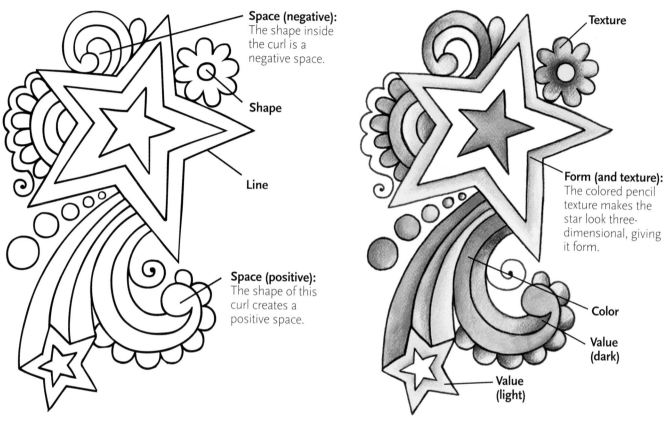

Space (negative): The shape inside the curl is a negative space.

Shape

Line

Space (positive): The shape of this curl creates a positive space.

Texture

Form (and texture): The colored pencil texture makes the star look three-dimensional, giving it form.

Color

Value (dark)

Value (light)

Coloring Technique Ideas

Watercolors

Colored pencils layered over watercolors

Fine-point black pen layered over markers

Get Inspired by COLOR

When it comes to expressing emotion, there's no better way to express how you're feeling—or how you want someone else to feel—than through the use of color. Just think of some of your favorite memories and how they make you feel. I bet color plays a big part of what you remember. Whether it's a beautiful sunset, the green of spring after a long, cold winter, or a perfectly clean, white expanse of snow, color makes a huge impact on us, both visually and emotionally. Just look at the way different colors can give the same flower drawing a completely different feel.

I've found that planning is key when working with color. If you're like me and you just **love** color, it might seem a bit overwhelming to get started. There are just so many color choices! And it's easy to fall into the rut of using the same colors over and over again, just because you like them. Making color decisions before you start can make you feel comfortable using new colors. Plus, you won't have to make a choice when you're in the midst of coloring and decide you don't like the result as much as you thought you would. A great way to try some new color combinations is to take a few minutes—it won't take long!—to create your own palettes before you get started.

Here's a fun trick I've learned for making palettes. It works especially well if you're using markers or colored pencils. Lay out all of your markers (or pencils) on a table or floor so you can see every single color you have. Pick one favorite marker (pencil) that will serve as the **anchor color** for your palette. Make it a color you really enjoy working with (or for a challenge, maybe a color you never work with). Now, pick two or three other markers (pencils) that complement your anchor color and place those next to your anchor color to start building a palette. Keep going until you have picked five or six colors. At this point, you don't even have to use them—you're just putting them side-by-side to see how the colors look together. Keep adding or switching colors until you like what you see. It's so easy to swap different colors in and out this way. Once you have a group of colors that you like, test them out on paper to make sure you still like the way they look together. If you love it, be sure to create a sample page with the names of the markers/colors you used so you won't forget. This is a great way to quickly create a whole library of color palettes for yourself.

Another great place to get color inspiration is literally from the world around you. Color is everywhere—your clothing, your bag, even a tissue box—there are probably patterns and designs with interesting color palettes surrounding you now! I'm sure there are things you bought because you liked the colors, so use those things that you love as inspiration. I once bought a pack of hair elastics simply because they had the most beautiful combination of blues and purples. Almost anything, anywhere, can become a color inspiration, so always keep your eyes open!

A SPECTRUM of Emotion

Color can be a great way to express yourself and define your mood. When you sit down to color, ask yourself, "How do I feel today? How can I use color to express that feeling?" Sometimes you might even feel something you can't quite put into words, but you can express it with color.

I've included some of my favorite palettes on the following pages. Each one is paired with the emotion that best describes how the color combination makes me feel. But keep in mind that everyone is different, and that's what makes art so exciting. I love to use bright colors, but maybe you like more subdued colors. My "relaxed" palette might be your "cozy." There is no right or wrong when it comes to color! Use these palettes as a starting point and see how they make you feel. Try adding or taking away a color to customize the palette to reflect your taste and style. Then, make your own page full of YOUR favorite color palettes!

The next few pages contain some colored examples. Along the bottom edge of each page, I've included a palette with each individual color, shown separately, so you can easily match your marker, pencil, or paint colors to the colors I used.

Whether you use one of my palettes or create your own, always be sure the colors you choose reflect who you are and how you're feeling.

The circles along the outer edge of the gallery pieces show you each individual color I used in that particular piece. If you like the palette I chose, you can use these circles to match the colors of your own pencils or markers.

The circles along the bottom of the gallery pieces show you which colors are more dominant in each design. The larger the circle, the more dominant the color. The smaller circles show tints and shades of a main color that were introduced for variety.

Take the COLOR WHEEL for a Spin!

A lot of times, simply following your feelings will lead you right to your color choices, but sometimes you might get stuck, and that's OK! Maybe you just don't know what you're feeling or you want to try something different with color and aren't sure where to start. The color wheel can be an awesome guide to help you make color choices.

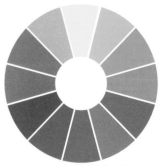

The Color Wheel

The color wheel is a visual guide to the relationships between colors based on their position on the wheel. When placed together, certain colors look harmonious while others might clash. It all depends on the relationship of the colors to one another. Each color in a palette needs to be surrounded by the right companions to shine!

The color wheel diagrams below are a great starting place to find colors that will automatically look lovely together. But always remember, the color wheel is only a guide. Feel free to add more colors to a palette or take some away. The best color choices are always the ones that reflect how you're feeling and what makes you happy. Have fun!

Complementary Colors
Complementary colors are pairs of opposites. They are directly across from one another on the color wheel.

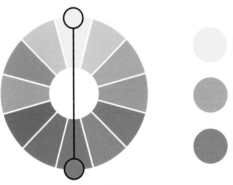

Complementary Colors

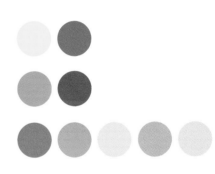

Palette Ideas

Split Complementary Colors
A split complementary color palette is created when one color is grouped with the two colors on either side of its complementary color.

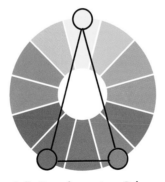

Split Complementary Colors

Palette Ideas

Analogous Colors
Analogous color palettes are created by choosing several colors that sit right next to each other on the color wheel.

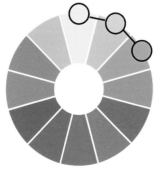

Analogous Colors

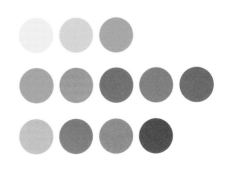

Palette Ideas

Triadic Colors

Triadic means "group of three." Triadic palettes are created by choosing any three colors that are equally spaced on the color wheel.

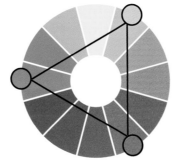

Triadic Colors

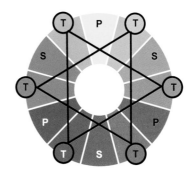

Palette Ideas

Examples of Triadic Color Palettes

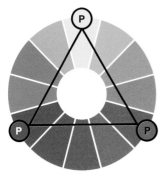

Primary

The three primary colors (red, yellow, and blue) form a triadic palette when grouped together.

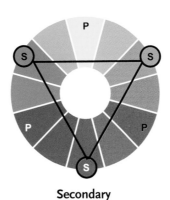

Secondary

Secondary colors are the colors directly in between the primary colors on the color wheel. When you shift the triangle around the wheel by two spaces, you've found the secondary colors.

Tertiary

Tertiary colors fall in between the primary and secondary colors. These are some of my favorite colors to work with!

Tetradic Colors

Tetradic means "group of four." Using a rectangle or square to choose colors on the color wheel is a fun way to instantly create a group of four colors that look great together. Both use two sets of complementary colors. Try rotating the rectangle or square around the wheel to create many different palettes.

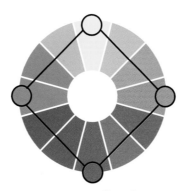

Square Tetradic Colors

Palette Ideas

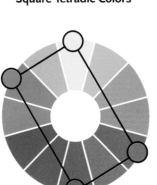

Rectangle Tetradic Colors

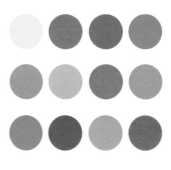

Palette Ideas

A SPECTRUM of Emotion

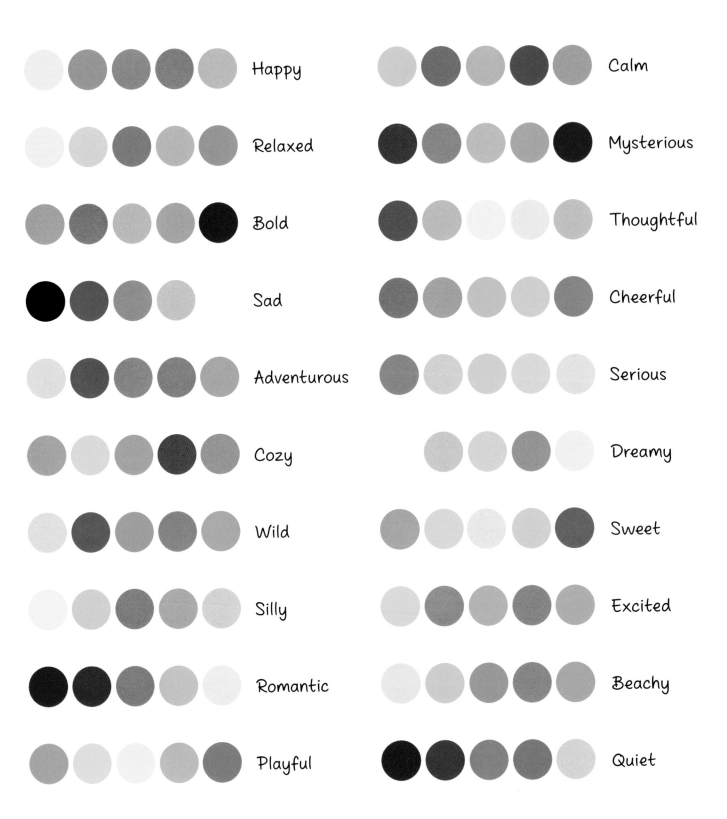

Happy

Relaxed

Bold

Sad

Adventurous

Cozy

Wild

Silly

Romantic

Playful

Calm

Mysterious

Thoughtful

Cheerful

Serious

Dreamy

Sweet

Excited

Beachy

Quiet

If there is magic on this planet,
it is contained in water.

—Loren Eiseley

We do not find the meaning of life by ourselves alone—we find it with another.

—Thomas Merton

The most beautiful thing we can experience
is the mysterious. It is the source of all
true art and science.

—Albert Einstein

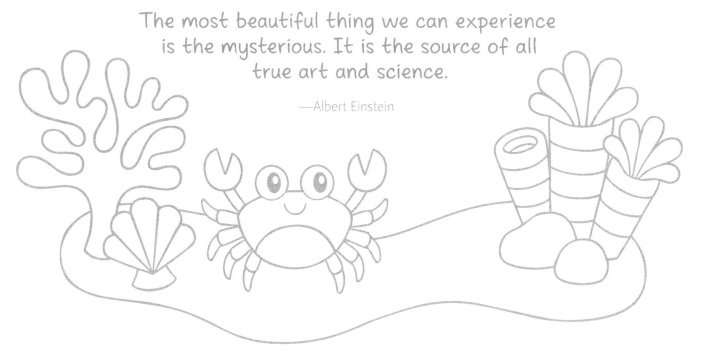

The ocean is everything I want
to be. Beautiful, mysterious,
wild and free.

—Unknown

No human being, however great, or
powerful, was ever so free as a fish.

—John Ruskin

For whatever we lose (like a you or a me), it's always ourselves we find in the sea.

—E.E. Cummings

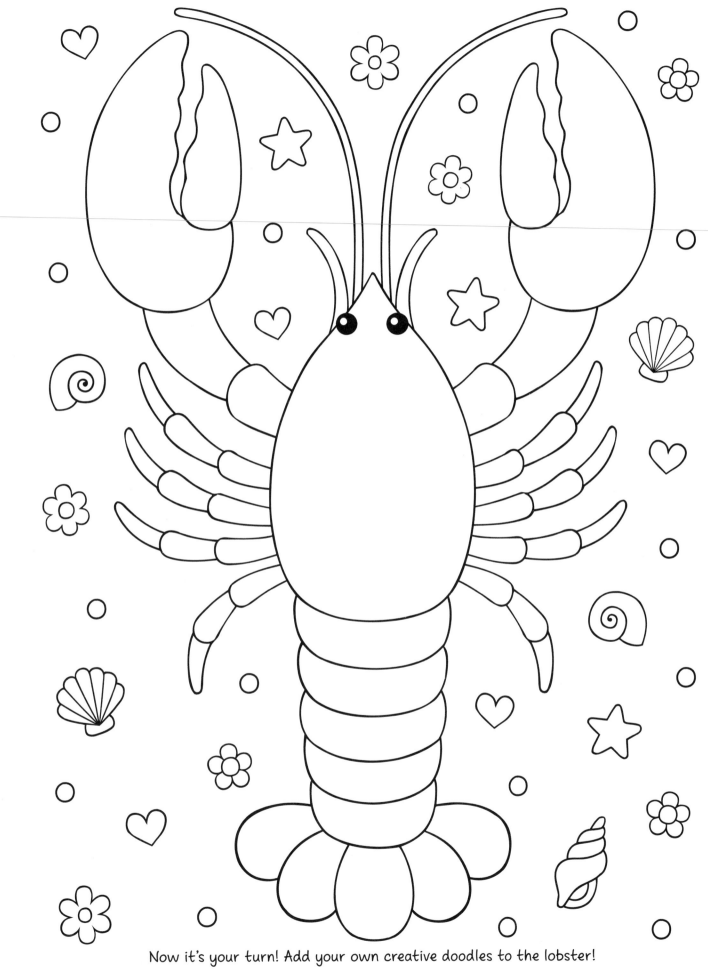

Now it's your turn! Add your own creative doodles to the lobster!

I go to nature to be soothed and healed,
and to have my senses put in order.

—John Burroughs

Not all stars belong to the sky.

—Unknown

We do not see nature with
our eyes, but with our
understandings and our hearts.

—William Hazlitt

Nobody can conceive or imagine all
the wonders there are unseen and
unseeable in the world.

—Francis P. Church

Together we can face challenges
as deep as the ocean and as
high as the sky.

—Sonia Gandhi

Individually, we are one drop.
Together, we are an ocean.

—Ryunosuke Satoro

If you want to hear the distant voice of the ocean put your ear to the lips of a seashell.

—Curtis Tyrone Jones

Have fun filling the seashells and starfish with your own doodley designs!

One cannot collect all the beautiful
shells on the beach.

—Anne Morrow Lindbergh

Don't sit and wait. Get out
there, feel life. Touch the sun,
and immerse in the sea.

—Rumi

The sea is everything. ... It is
an immense desert, where man
is never lonely, for he feels life
stirring on all sides.

—Jules Verne

Dive deep for the treasure
that you seek.

—Unknown

I wish I was an octopus, so I could hug 10 people at a time!

—Drew Barrymore

The whales do not sing because
they have an answer, they sing
because they have a song.

—Gregory Colbert

In order for the light
to shine so brightly, the
darkness must be present.

—Francis Bacon

You can't stop the waves, but
you can learn to surf.

—Jon Kabat-Zinn

The sea is a desert of waves,
A wilderness of water.

—Langston Hughes

To find a seashell is to discover a world of imagination.

—Michelle Held

The sea is as near as we come to another world.

—Anne Stevenson

Though we travel the world over to find the beautiful, we must carry it with us or we find it not.

—Ralph Waldo Emerson

What is any ocean but a
multitude of drops?

—David Mitchell

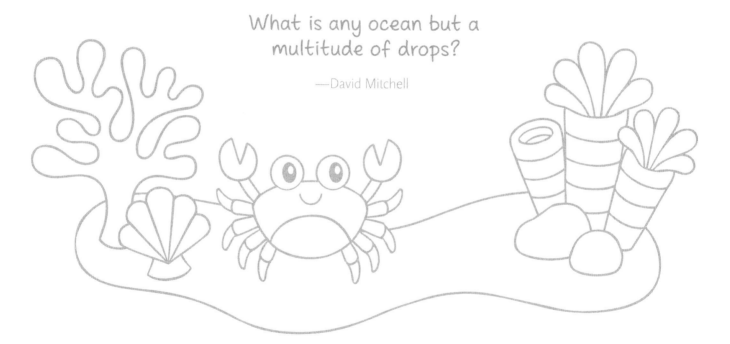

Add your own fun doodles to the turtle, seashells, starfish, and sand dollar!

With every drop of water you
drink, every breath you take,
you're connected to the sea.

—Sylvia Earle

Those who dwell among the beauties and mysteries of the earth are never alone or weary of life.

—Rachel Carson

In all things of nature there is
something of the marvelous.

—Aristotle

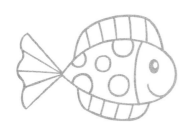

Every seashell has a story.

—Unknown

The sea, once it casts its
spell, holds one in its net of
wonder forever.

—Jacques Cousteau